SONG *of*
SILENCE

SONG *of* ❦ SILENCE

The Journey of Saint Jeanne Jugan

Éloi Leclerc

Translated from the French
by Claire Trocmé

auline
BOOKS & MEDIA
Boston

Library of Congress Cataloging-in-Publication Data

Leclerc, Eloi.
    [Jeanne Jugan. English]
    Song of silence : the journey of Saint Jeanne Jugan / Eloi Leclerc ; translated from
the French by Claire Trocmé. – 1st North American ed.
        p. cm.
    Originally published: The desert and the rose. London : Darton, Longman, and
Todd, c2002.
    ISBN 0-8198-8319-0 (pbk.)
    1. Jugan, Jeanne, 1792?-1879. 2. Little Sisters of the Poor–Biography. I. Title.
    BX4403.8.L4313 2009
    282.092–dc22
    [B]

                                                                2009023036

Unless otherwise noted, the Scripture quotations contained herein are from the *New Revised Standard Version Bible: Catholic Edition*, copyright © 1989, 1993, Division of Christian Education of the National Council of the Churches of Christ in the United States of America. Used by permission. All rights reserved.

Additional Scripture texts in this work are taken from the *New American Bible with Revised New Testament and Revised Psalms* © 1991, 1986, 1970 Confraternity of Christian Doctrine, Washington, D.C. and are used by permission of the copyright owner. All Rights Reserved. No part of the *New American Bible* may be reproduced in any form without permission in writing from the copyright owner.

Cover design by Rosana Usselmann

Cover photo by Mary Emmanuel Alves, FSP

Photos courtesy of the Little Sisters of the Poor.

"P" and PAULINE are registered trademarks of the Daughters of St. Paul.

Originally published in French in 2000 under the title *Jeanne Jugan: Le Désert et la Rose* by Desclée de Brouwer, Paris.

Copyright © 2002, Éloi Leclerc. Published by Darton, Longman, and Todd Ltd. London, UK.

First North American Edition published by Daughters of St. Paul, Boston, MA.

Published by Pauline Books & Media, 50 Saint Paul's Avenue, Boston, MA 02130-3491
www.pauline.org

Printed in the U.S.A.

Pauline Books & Media is the publishing house of the Daughters of St. Paul, an international congregation of women religious serving the Church with the communications media.

1 2 3 4 5 6 7 8 9   13 12 11 10 09

Who is that coming up from the wilderness,
leaning upon her beloved?
(SONG OF SOLOMON 8:5)

Who is this that looks forth like the dawn?
(SONG OF SOLOMON 6:10)

Contents

Foreword

DURING THE MORE THAN 150 years since the founding of the Little Sisters of the Poor, Saint Jeanne Jugan's commitment to service has been maintained with the same care and devotion that she showed in welcoming the poor elderly of Saint-Servan to her simple abode. The Little Sisters excel in continuing the ministry established by their foundress and upholding the original charism.

The contemporary world needs the example of Saint Jeanne Jugan. We need to be awakened from our obsession with material success, social achievement, and the seemingly endless accumulation of things. We need to provide the time and space in our lives that will allow us to recognize the presence of Jesus in our brothers and sisters, especially the poor, the frail, and those who have no one to care for them.

At the time Saint Jeanne and her emerging community were caring for senior citizens, it would not have been imagined that we would see so many people living into their eighties, nineties, and even the beginning of their second century. Advances in medical care and better standards of living allow us to live well beyond the life expectancy of previous generations. On the whole we live much longer, but we do not always live better or have the care and companionship we need. Jesus' public ministry was often directed to renewing people and restoring them to their place in the community; helping them to find meaning in their lives. Saint Jeanne Jugan and the Sisters who carry on her work follow Jesus' example as they renew and restore the forgotten elderly, those who find themselves alone and without basic needs. They are light in the darkness for women and men who are burdened by the demands of the senior years; they help our elderly brothers and sisters to find meaning and fulfillment each day.

Through this important chronicle of Saint Jeanne's life, with particular focus on her unquestioning trust in the will of God, Éloi Leclerc has provided us a window into Saint Jeanne's soul. As Pope John Paul II noted at Saint Jeanne's beatification, "she depended completely on Divine Providence, which she saw operative in her own life and in that of others," and she let that faith-filled confidence be a prompting to action, to going forth in the name of the Lord. The Church today needs people to embrace that kind of confidence and commitment, to take to heart Pope John Paul's recognition that Saint Jeanne's message is relevant for us here and now. The Church needs people to take their place among those actively witnessing to Jesus Christ, and not live their lives as members of a witness protection program. We need to be inspired by the bravery and selfless dedication of the prayerful young woman of Brittany.

As we go forth to build up the Church and a Culture of Life, we must not fail to recognize the fullness of human dignity in all people at all times, from the moment of their conception to the last moment of natural life. Aided by the intercession of Saint Jeanne Jugan, and calling to mind her fidelity and unquestioning trust in God's will, let us go forward to fulfill the mission given us by Jesus Christ as set forth in the twenty-fifth chapter of Matthew's Gospel: *Whatever you did for the least of your brethren, you did for me.*

Cardinal Seán P. O'Malley, O.F.M. Cap.

Archbishop of Boston

Introduction

WRITTEN DURING A STAY WITH the Little Sisters of the Poor, in the land of corsairs,[1] the following pages take in the inner world and the high seas in the same sweep of the eye. They tell the story of a seafarer's daughter from Cancale.[2] The tale is intimate yet open to immensity, an adventure more exhilarating than a round-the-world sail. We are swept away by it, far, far from the pettiness and gossip of the moment. On a starless night, making way across invisible seas, we reach new lands and discover lives unknown—our own. Our lives in their full depth, our lives set free, transfigured. In a word, our true lives.

---

1. Corsairs were privateers commissioned by sea traders to ensure the safety of their ships as they brought goods into port. Their duties might extend to attacking and seizing foreign merchant ships, considered enemies of the state,. The Breton port of Saint-Malo was home to a number of corsairs, one of whom was ennobled by King Louis XIV of France in 1708. They made a lasting mark on the culture of the region (Translator's note).

2. Cancale is a small fishing port on the northern coast of Brittany, in western France.

Some destinies speak to us more than others. They are beacons on our way, prompting us to dream of greater things. We can see in them something of ourselves, but greater, and freer. Those men and women who hold a fascination for us were themselves subject to our human condition with its contradictions, its darkness, its tragedy. By opening it up to the light, however, they lead us onward, illuminate us, and cause us to grow. They make us realize that we are carried and nourished by a reality that is deeper than the outside world.

Yet at first sight, everything in the lives of these men and women seems to distance them from us. They appear as heroes, superhuman beings. They launch into extraordinary enterprises. They show exceptional courage, boldness, and selflessness. They accomplish feats the likes of which we would not even conceive. They stand fast where "we would have arrived only to stumble straight away."[3] All in all, they are worth a hundred times more than we are.

Then suddenly they are beset by difficulties, battered by storms. We find them halted in their creative endeavor, rendered powerless, stripped, abandoned, as if thrown to the ground. They are spared nothing. They end up being treated as the least of human beings, as the weakest among us. "Here is the man!" says Pilate as he shows to the crowd the powerless Christ, whipped, covered in blood, spat upon, ridiculed. The man indeed. Only the man is left, stripped of any glory, of any persona, of any status or protection. The man, abandoned to poverty, to solitude, to darkness.

---

3. Paul Claudel, "Saint François," *Oeuvre poétique* (Paris: Gallimard La Pléiade, 1957).

The poverty, solitude, and darkness into which these men and women are plunged are familiar to us; indeed, they are ours. Yet as these people take on our darkest lot, they transform it into a path of light. We can feel ourselves grow with them.

From that point of view, the life of Jeanne Jugan, foundress of the Little Sisters of the Poor, is illuminating:

> On the face of it all this foundress's activities are crowded into the space of three or four years. For those few years, she is and does everything. Everything begins with and from her: not only the first foundation, but those immediately born from it. If one begins to wilt, Jeanne Jugan is sent, Jeanne Jugan rushes to the rescue. She is the one to whom everyone turns; she is the one whom the public know and admire. But soon, her true role stops being an official one. And then, suddenly, she disappears. For the remaining quarter of a century of her life, she is nothing to anyone, not even to her own congregation. Miraculously forgotten, you might say.... Forgotten for a quarter of a century.... [4]

Such an experience challenges us. At first, there is the attraction, the desire to accomplish a great work of a sort that can only be accomplished with creative enthusiasm. A work that mobilizes, inspires, and multiplies all the human creative energies and that, in spite of the difficulties encountered, exalts human capabilities by giving one the feeling of working with God, of doing God's work. Creating a great human and divine work always stimulates enthusiasm. It is being a creator with God.

---

4. Gabriel-Marie Garrone, *Poor in Spirit: The Spirituality of Jeanne Jugan* (London: Darton, Longman, and Todd, 1977), 12–13.

Then, suddenly, God seems to lose interest, if not in the work itself, at least in the one he chose to accomplish it. The chosen one is left alone by the roadside, forgotten, rejected. This is the desert experience, the void. An affecting moment when a whole life may plunge into bitterness, resentment, and revolt.

Nothing is more dramatic than this encounter of a human being with God's silence in the experience of the inner void. In those depths is the true drama of humanity played out. Nothing is decided in advance, nor can anything be taken for granted. We believe that God had called us to accomplish a work, a great work. And here we are, asked to be dispossessed of that work in order to become God's work ourselves: "In vain do you attempt this or that; it is really you, poor little brother, who are wanted."[5]

God does not force himself on us. When he wants to make his dwelling in his creature and to make himself known in the fullness of his love, he waits for consent—total, unreserved, unconditional consent. This presupposes a complete relinquishing of the self, which does not happen without resistance. It is Jacob's fight with the angel in the night. God asks human beings to let go, to give up every possible support, every certainty, to go out of our depth, so to speak. Oh, how hard it is totally to put our trust in Another, when our fate is in the balance! As long as we persist in staying at the helm of our destiny, we are under the impression that we exist of our own volition. Letting go would appear to be suicide. So God waits. Until dawn.

---

5. Claudel, "Saint François."

This unique experience makes plain the way God, the Infinite Being, enters a human existence and becomes one with a finite being, without substituting himself to that finite being.

Such an encounter can only occur in the deepest inner solitude. The individual is, as it were, left to his own devices, with every support taken away. Alone with free will, the seeker grapples with the Infinite Reality, until the moment when freely accepted dispossession gives way to ineffable communion. Then a new birth takes place. In the depths of the being, a hidden source begins to sing. God's tenderness fills his creature's heart:

> Underneath it all, You see that there is in me something holy, something very small, O my God, which looks to You in faith.
>
> Listen! Something that cries out to You ceaselessly, night and day!
>
> Something stronger that tries to lift itself up towards You ...
>
> There is in me such thirst for Your tenderness and sweetness ...
>
> Turn Your face towards me! Father, look inside Your child! Ah, this child, will You say, this little child and My maidservant's child![6]

The reader may have guessed that my intention is not to write a biography of Jeanne Jugan. There are some excellent ones, which faithfully tell her life's story. The following pages are an approach to her inner experience from the time she was condemned to inaction, silence, and solitude. I follow her to La Tour Saint-Joseph; I aim to enter her

---

6. Paul Claudel, "Psalm 85."

solitude, listen to her silence, perceive its inner turmoil, its deep resonance.

To this end I pored over the testimonies of the Little Sisters of the Poor and of people who came close to Jeanne during her long stay at La Tour. I collected the statements they gave at the beatification hearing.[7]

As I heard these testimonies and allowed them to resonate in me, I felt drawn by the depth of a life. What I was discovering was not only the calm after the storm, a smooth sea, as if asleep; it was also the bubbling of waters which, under the powerful force of the Spirit, gave birth to a new creation.

---

7. *Jeanne Jugan: Positio super virtutibus*, Congregation for the Causes of Saints, Rome, 1976.

Brief Chronology

October 25, 1792	Jeanne Jugan is born at Cancale (Ille-et-Vilaine) France.
April 1796	Her father is lost at sea.
1801	The Concordat between Church and state restores religious peace in France after the French Revolution.
1803	Presumed year of Jeanne's first Holy Communion.
1810	Jeanne serves Viscountess de la Choue as a kitchen maid.
1816	Jeanne turns down a marriage proposal from a Cancalais sailor. She tells her mother: "God wants me for himself. He is keeping me for a work that is still unknown...."

1817	Jeanne leaves Cancale for Saint-Servan. She joins the staff of the Le Rosais Hospital as a nursing assistant.
1823	Exhaustion forces her to leave Le Rosais. She is taken on by Mlle Lecoq of Saint-Servan, who welcomes her as a friend rather than a maid. Together the two women visit the poor.
1835	Mlle Lecoq dies. Jeanne works part time for other well-to-do families in the area.
1837–1838	With a friend, Françoise Aubert, Jeanne rents a flat on the second floor of No. 2, Rue du Centre, in Saint-Servan.
Winter 1839	With her two companions, Françoise Aubert and Virginie Trédaniel, Jeanne takes in a blind and infirm elderly woman, Anne Chauvin. She gives Anne her own bed and goes to live in the attic. A second person is taken in shortly afterward. Virginie Trédaniel and a friend, Marie Jamet, assist Jeanne. This is the humble beginning of a great work. Jeanne is 47 years old.
December 1840	Madeleine Bourges, a sick, young working girl, comes to be looked after by Jeanne. After her recovery, she joins Virginie and Marie.
October 1841	Jeanne and her companions, with their guests, leave the flat at the Rue du

Centre for less constricted accommodation—a ground-floor flat in the Rue de la Fontaine.

1841–1842   With the support and advice of the Brothers Hospitallers of Saint John of God, Jeanne starts collecting for the poor.

February 1842   Requests for admission from the elderly increase continually. Jeanne and her followers acquire the former convent of the Daughters of the Cross.

May 1842   Jeanne is elected superior of the small association, in the presence of Father Auguste Le Pailleur, curate of the parish of Saint-Servan. A rule is drawn up, inspired by the Rule of the Brothers Hospitallers of Saint John of God. The name "Servants of the Poor" is adopted.

October 1842   Marie Jamet leaves home to join the small association, bringing to four the number of the "Servants of the Poor."

December 1843   Jeanne is re-elected as superior. Father Le Pailleur, on his own authority, annuls the election and puts Marie Jamet in her place.

1844   The "Servants of the Poor" change their name to "Sisters of the Poor."

1845   Jeanne is awarded the Montyon Prize by the Academié Française for her work.

1845–1846 The news is widely reported in the national and local press.

1846 Jeanne collects in Rennes, where a house is founded. Jeanne goes to Dinan, where she opens a third house. The English author Charles Dickens visits. Jeanne Jugan is commended several times by the press in Rennes and Dinan.

1847 A house is founded in Tours.

The first general chapter of the Sisters of the Poor is held. Jeanne is not invited.

September 1848 A long article on Jeanne's work by Louis Veuillot appears on the front page of a Catholic daily newspaper, *L'Univers*, published in Paris.

1848 The motherhouse and novitiate are established in Tours.

1849 Jeanne lives in Tours.

Foundations are established in Paris, Nantes, and Besançon.

The popular name "Little Sisters of the Poor" is definitively adopted.

1850 Jeanne founds a house in Angers.

Houses are opened in Bordeaux, Rouen, Nancy …

The Little Sisters number more than 100, including novices and postulants.

1851	First foundation in England.
1852	The motherhouse and novitiate return to Rennes. Jeanne is also recalled to Rennes. She is ordered to cease all activity and break all sustained contact with benefactors. It is the start of her long retirement.
1853	First foundation in Belgium.
1854	The congregation numbers 500 Little Sisters in thirty-six houses.
1856	On January 30, the estate of La Tour Saint-Joseph in the village of Saint-Pern (Ille-et-Vilaine) is acquired. The motherhouse and novitiate move there in early April. Jeanne goes as well. Relegated to living among the novices and postulants, she shares their life until her death.
1863	First foundation in Spain.
1866	The Saint-Servan town council names the street of the House of the Cross after Jeanne Jugan.
1867	One-hundredth foundation, in Toulon.
1868	First foundations in Ireland, the United States, and North Africa.
1869	First foundation in Italy.
1879	Pope Leo XIII approves the constitutions of the congregation, now numbering 2,400 Little Sisters, for a period of seven years.

August 28, 1879	Death of Jeanne Jugan, aged 86, at La Tour Saint-Joseph.
October 3, 1982	Pope John Paul II beatifies Jeanne Jugan.
October 11, 2009	Pope Benedict XVI canonizes Jeanne Jugan.

CHAPTER I

Over There

O N April 1, 1856, three Little Sisters of the Poor arrived from Rennes at the manor of La Tour, in Saint-Pern (in the département of Ille-et-Vilaine). Their newly founded institute had just acquired that large estate, formerly the property of the Comte de Saint-Pern and situated approximately nineteen miles northwest of Rennes. It being the feast day of Saint Joseph, the Little Sisters named the estate La Tour Saint-Joseph.

Their eyes opened wide with surprise as they discovered the vast and superb estate: a land of hills and vales, of woods and water, with beautiful avenues of lime trees and magnificent gardens. There were even ponds powering small water mills.

From then on this was where the motherhouse and the novitiate of their congregation would be located. With the number of novices constantly on the increase, a large house of formation was needed to welcome them. Twenty-seven were expected at the end of the month. The same number of postulants would follow.

Toward the end of April, Jeanne Jugan, foundress of the congregation, also arrived at La Tour. She came from Rennes, where she had spent four years behind the walls of La Piletière. She was arriving, no longer as foundress, but stripped of any title and authority, divested of all duties and responsibilities, like the least of the sisters.

Four years previously, Father Auguste Le Pailleur, adviser to the community from the beginning, had obtained his bishop's approval for its statutes. This approval officially made the priest superior general of the Little Sisters of the Poor.

Le Pailleur's first decision had been to call Jeanne, the foundress of the order, barely sixty years old and fully active, to the motherhouse in Rennes. He asked her to cease all transactions, collecting [of charity], and sustained contact with benefactors. She was in future to consider herself a mere sister, relieved of any authority and responsibility.[1]

Jeanne, the great traveler, the indefatigable collector, the charismatic woman who had set off throughout the world a great wave of solidarity with the poor and the elderly, she who was admired by all, was now to remain quiet, hidden, and forgotten. She would hereafter be known only by her religious name, Soeur Marie de la Croix (Sister Mary of the Cross).

---

1. As early as 1843, Father Le Pailleur had on his own authority annulled Jeanne's reelection and imposed as superior his spiritual daughter, Marie Jamet.

Jeanne had obeyed without protest. In the future, everything in the congregation would be decided without reference to her. All she was being asked to do was to let herself be forgotten. Four years had gone by in this way in the shadows and silence of La Piletière in Rennes. Now, in April 1856, Sister Mary of the Cross was on her way to La Tour.

Four and a half hours' journey by coach at the speed of a jogging horse gives one plenty of time to reflect and meditate. The farther she traveled from Rennes and the deeper the track penetrated into the solitude of the countryside, the better Jeanne could form an idea of what her new life would be like. In Rennes, she would have been able to go out into town now and again to shop or to make a few visits. She would have been able to meet friendly acquaintances. Over there, at La Tour, even those things would be impossible. She had understood quickly what was being asked of her: simply to be there, away from the town, far from any contact; in short, far from everything, hidden in the country as if buried alive.

Yet she went without the least bitterness, serene but aware, fully aware. One thing comforted her: she was traveling with the postulants. She had always loved the young. She would be among them; she could help them, contribute to their formation, and, if need be, counsel them. It had been made clear that at La Tour she would not reside in the part of the buildings set aside for the ruling authorities of the congregation, but that she would throw in her lot with the novices.

During the journey from Rennes to Saint-Pern, Jeanne had all the time in the world to contemplate the countryside as it unfurled slowly under her gaze. It was early spring, and nature was coming back to life. Meadows grew green, and trees were covered in brand-new foliage. Where farmers were plowing the fields, the silent soil allowed itself to be turned over and broken, in readiness for receiving the seed. Jeanne observed that process thoughtfully. Was that not what the Lord expected of her now? That she let herself be turned over, broken, so that she might become loose, open soil? Although everything might be taken from her, she still had her heart—the capacity for love and wonder, which was so deep in her. Nor could anything or anyone prevent her from opening herself up more and more to this abundance. The swell of her heart would keep growing deeper, to rise higher.

Jeanne was sixty-four. She still felt rich in inner resources and capable of undertaking great things. Her youthful dream was alive in her heart. "God wants me for himself. He is keeping me for a work as yet unknown," she had told her mother when a young sailor from Cancale had repeatedly proposed marriage to her. Her dream had come true. A new and wonderful work had sprung from her heart and hands. The seed had germinated and grown beyond all expectation. It was a work that met the needs of her time and was admired by the elite of society, saluted by such renowned journalists as Louis Veuillot. Vocations were plentiful, new foundations multiplied. A growing number of the poor and the elderly were being helped. The new institute of the Little Sisters of the Poor spread over the world the great mantle of God's gentle pity. That was the nature of Jeanne's heart.

The adventure had started humbly one winter's night in 1839, when Jeanne was forty-seven years old. She lived in Saint-Servan,[2] not far from the church of Sainte-Croix, in a dwelling she shared with two female companions. The three women lived a communal life of sorts, punctuated by prayer. Jeanne worked a few hours here and there. In her comings and goings, she could not but notice the destitution of countless poor people. At a time when no formal welfare existed, poverty-stricken elderly people were often found abandoned on the streets. In 1832 the city's charity office helped 2,000 paupers. Five years later, the number was close to 3,500.

The population of Saint-Servan was then between 9,000 and 10,000, many of them seafarers. Too often decimated by tragedies at sea, they left elderly parents without resources. The city had neither hospice nor any other place where the elderly poor could be taken in, and many old people were exposed to all sorts of hardship.

Jeanne could see this distress. She had always been sensitive to the sufferings of the less fortunate. Before living near the church of Sainte-Croix, she had looked after patients at the hospital of Le Rosais for six years. What was she to do in the face of this tide of human suffering? She could not contemplate setting up a welfare organization. Distress could not wait.

Jeanne acted immediately, concretely, responding to her womanly heart. At the first cold weather of winter in 1839 she decided, in agreement with her two companions, to bring home an elderly woman who was paralyzed and

---

2. Situated near Saint-Malo, Saint-Servan is today part of that city.

blind. Jeanne settled the woman in her own bedroom, while she went up to sleep in the attic.

It was a small thing in the face of immense human distress, yet it was the start of a great adventure. Soon another poor woman was taken in. Encouraged by the Brothers Hospitallers of Saint John of God, Jeanne started collecting money from families who were known to her. Drawn by her example, young women who wished, as she did, to help the needy poor came to offer their services and joined the three able-bodied women.

This was the start of a charitable association that adopted a rule of life inspired by the Third Order founded by Saint John Eudes. Jeanne belonged to this Third Order and received inner nourishment from its spirituality. She liked to contemplate the love of God, as revealed in the Hearts of Jesus and Mary. Thus she opened herself up to the source of the great love that was to fill her life and that, through her, would spread over the world.

The small community and its life project soon found support from the young curate of the parish of Saint-Servan, Auguste Le Pailleur, who became its adviser.

The community, which was growing constantly, started to search for larger premises. After a short stay in a ground-floor accommodation in the Rue de la Fontaine, "the Big Downstairs," it moved into the former convent of the Daughters of the Cross. On May 29, 1842, gathered around Father Le Pailleur, this association of women spelled out its rules and chose Jeanne as its superior.

The small charitable association was gradually turning into a religious community. Then came a great leap forward, a veritable cascade of foundations. Houses opened one after the other in towns around France: Rennes, Dinan, Tours, Paris, Nantes, Besançon. The number of sisters was growing constantly. In 1851, the tally stood at 300 sisters, fifteen houses, 1,500 elderly people housed and helped. Jeanne proved tireless; she went from town to town, opening a house here, rushing there to the rescue of a foundation in trouble. She was everywhere, answering every call.

Such expansion of the work could not but attract the attention of the highest authorities in the land. In 1845, the Académie Française awarded Jeanne the Montyon Prize, under the dome,[3] in the presence of an illustrious audience including François-René de Chateaubriand, Alphonse de Lamartine, Victor Hugo, Adolphe Thiers, François Guizot, and Charles Augustin Sainte-Beuve. André Dupin closed the customary speech with this litany of praise: "How could Jeanne meet such expense? What shall I say to you, gentlemen? Providence is great. Jeanne is indefatigable; Jeanne is eloquent; Jeanne has prayers; Jeanne has tears; Jeanne has work; Jeanne has her basket, which she always carries on her arm, and which she always brings back full. Saintly soul! The Académie places in that basket the amount it has available: it awards you a prize of 3,000 francs!"

Now Jeanne was going *over there* so that she might be forgotten. Reduced to inaction, silence, and solitude by the one who had advised her but had suddenly decided to take her place and award himself the title of Founder.

Jeanne was certainly not a woman who would allow herself to be trampled on, always ready to give in for the sake

---

3. The dome of the former Mazarin College chapel in Paris, where formal ceremonies of the Académie Française still take place (Translator's note).

of peace. Born in Cancale, the daughter of a fisherman, accustomed to a rugged life from her earliest years, she had extraordinary energy, "wonderfully served by gentle and imperturbable tenacity." She knew what she wanted. She was the typical Cancalaise woman: tall, determined, combining the allure of a lofty figure with a decisive personality, ready to face whatever might come. Add to this a practical intelligence, ever alert, and an ability to adapt, as if instinctively, to the most unpredictable situations.

Yet, as she traveled through the Breton countryside toward the solitude of La Tour at Saint-Pern, Jeanne was in no way tempted to rebel, to protest and claim what was hers by right. What was happening within her?

Jeanne had never set much store by her own person, or titles, or fame. She carried her treasure within her. Her will for good and her capacity for love were her great strengths, her treasure. The rest mattered little. In any case, her collecting rounds for the elderly had taught her to stamp on her own pride. They had been a true school for renouncing complacency. Jeanne would later confide as much to a young sister at La Tour: "You may one day be sent our collecting. It will cost you. I did it too, and it cost me; I did it for God, for the poor."

She was once slapped by a rich man. Without losing her calm, Jeanne said to him, "Thank you! That slap was for me. Now, please give me something for my poor." Assaults on her person did not count. Only the poor counted, those who had to be helped and made happy.

On another occasion, Jeanne had presented herself at the charity office of the town of Saint-Servan, as she often did, to receive the bread for her elderly people. Out of respect for her, when the time came for distribution, she was usually allowed to enter into the courtyard of the building, which gave her precedence and saved her from mixing with the professional beggars. But on that day the employee, being ill-disposed, spat out at her: "Get into line, like the others!" For that employee, Jeanne was not there "for them," for the needy. She was, quite simply, one of them. She must see herself as such, a poor woman, and therefore take her place in the line of beggars. Jeanne got the message. It was not enough to be the *servant* of the poor, the woman who made collections for her poor; she had to be the *little sister* of the poor. Poor with the poor.

Such was the road along which the Lord led her toward greater selflessness. He helped her to discover true value and greatness in the capacity for love, in the inexhaustible will for good he had placed in her heart as a sharing in divine generosity itself. Jeanne had built her life on this inner abundance. No one could take that away from her. Compared with it, everything else paled into insignificance.

There lay the secret of the peace and serenity she retained at the very moment when everything was unjustly taken from her. Forgotten, excluded even from the council[4] where she belonged, she might suffer, but she was not shaken. She would play the game of oblivion so well that those around her would end up not knowing she was the foundress and the first Little Sister of the Poor.

Yet in what was being asked of her now by way of renunciation, there was something unprecedented and entirely

---

4. The council was the governing body of the congregation [made up of the mother general and her assistants, Translator]. As founder, Jeanne was by rights a member of this council.

new. Until this point, her capacity for love had been translated into action. This action was often crucifying for her
ego, but it was nevertheless *her* action. She was acting in the
service of a great cause. Now this force for love would have
to be translated into pure consent for the action of
Another.

It was therefore not enough to serve the poor, to expend
herself for them body and soul, even at the cost of great
sacrifices. She needed to accept being poor herself: not to
hang onto action, but to let go, present herself before God
with empty, open hands, with a poor person's heart. Let
him do the action. In short, learn to be poor in love, especially in love.

This could only be achieved through a complete inner
turnaround. When Jeanne arrived at La Tour, the place of
her great solitude, in April 1856, the words she had said to
her mother so long before—"God wants me for himself, for
a work as yet unknown"—took on a new meaning, a truly
overwhelming meaning. Yes, God wanted her for himself,
more than ever; and more than ever "for a work as yet
unknown." This unknown work would be Jeanne herself. It
was no longer for her a matter of accomplishing work, but
of consenting to become God's work.

Being *over there*, forgotten by all, would be a long road
of silence, faith, and love. Day after day, for years on end,
alone with God, Jeanne would learn a form of divine
humility. The woman who had collected bread for the poor
would become God's collector, God's beggar. By way of
this light-filled shadow, she would come into the fullness of
God. Then being *over there* would be splendor.

CHAPTER 2

The Silence of the Rose

EVERY REGION, EVERY LANDSCAPE HAS its color, which varies with the seasons: color of sea or forest, of orchards or meadows. In Brittany, in springtime, large clusters of gorse or broom blossom in banks and hedgerows. In the April sun the countryside blazes with patches of pure gold. Walking along footpaths plumed with blossom, you feel surrounded by a magical light that envelops and penetrates. You breathe it in. Even silence is the color of gold.

Then there are other days, slate-gray, wet days, with that fine, persistent drizzle called the *crachin* in Breton. Or others when howling gales rush in from the ocean, chasing heavy, low clouds over a silent, thoughtful land.

In the spring of 1856, "the weather was superb," according to one who witnessed the very beginnings of the Little Sisters at La Tour:

Everything was beautiful in the valleys, on the hillsides, under the oaks and beeches of the avenues, by the pond, among those old gardens with the high arbors and tall yews repeating ancient legends, along the terraces planted with lime and pine trees, from where you overlooked the whole region. Everything, down to the ticktack of our mills, had a rural character. There were no roads other than the low tracks; in the hedged fields you lost your way, in the meadows you sank into mud.

Every day, with her rosary in one hand and a stick in the other, Jeanne wandered through the meadows and the woods. She immediately took to this rural setting. She admired the wooded hills, with their rocky escarpments and their plantations of pines, sweet chestnuts, and oaks. She readily lingered to contemplate the ponds shimmering in the sun like mirrors, and when she stepped under the oak trees the branches of which formed a high arch overhead, it was like entering a green cathedral.

Sometimes she was seen stopping to marvel at the flowers in the grounds. A rose drew her eye. A simple rose, without a name. The rose never speaks its name; it does not introduce itself. It is not concerned to know whether it is being looked at or admired. It simply flowers, pure reflection of a beauty that is beyond any name. Its brilliance is ecstasy, its silence, praise. Attentive, Jeanne seemed to be listening to the silence of the rose.

Soon the solitude of La Tour echoed with a thousand noises. The old manor house and its outbuildings became a construction site. The buildings that were unsuitable for use, the barns, sheds, and stables, must be demolished; others must be altered, new ones built. Naturally enough, the restoration work started with the manor itself, but new buildings were planned, to receive hundreds of novices. Pickaxes, spades, and hammers swung into action for many months. From dawn to dusk, all that could be heard were hammering and the rattle of carts bringing in stones or other materials—all the noisy activity of a construction site.

On Sundays or feast days silence was restored to La Tour. Then there were the days of clothing[1] or profession ceremonies, when parents, friends, priests, or villagers from the surrounding area came in numbers. On those occasions, Jeanne made herself as small and discreet as possible, trying not to show herself. She mixed with the least prominent sisters, and did it naturally, with great ease. No one noticed her.

Yet it was no easy thing for her to accept being a nobody, losing herself in the crowd of the forgotten, placing herself among the faceless, the voiceless, and the nameless.

On July 25, 1856, the bishop of Rennes came to bless the estate and receive the profession of twenty-three Little Sisters. As the General Chapter of the Congregation was due to take place at approximately the same date, the superiors of the forty houses converged on La Tour. A large crowd from the neighboring villages also wanted to join the sisters for the ceremony. The temporary chapel clearly being too small to hold everyone, an altar was set up in one of the wide alleys in the garden, under a large canvas tent. After the ceremony, the bishop, led by Father Ernest

---

1. Ceremonies during which postulants, on becoming novices, received the habit of a Little Sister of the Poor. These ceremonies were discontinued in the late 1960s after the Second Vatican Council (Translator's note).

Lelièvre, went on a tour of the estate. Then, "seated on the grass, at the center of a wide circle formed by the Little Sisters, as befitted a father with his family, he spoke unceasingly of the wonderful growth of the society and the fruit of its works."

Father Le Pailleur also spoke in his capacity as superior general. He addressed congratulations to the long-standing sisters who were present, naming each one and saluting them as pillars of the congregation. But he omitted Jeanne. She alone was forgotten. He uttered not a single word about her. Total silence, utter oblivion.

It was as if she no longer existed, had never existed. Jeanne, who was present, said nothing. The rose does not speak its name. Never mind whether it is seen or unseen. It simply flowers. Its silence is that of eternal beauty, which is beyond any name. It is seen by God. That is enough.

That night, before going to sleep, Jeanne was able to turn to the Lord and say to him in all truthfulness, with the psalmist:

> O LORD, my heart is not lifted up,
>> my eyes are not raised too high;
> I do not occupy myself with things
>> too great and too marvelous for me.
> But I have calmed and quieted my soul,
>> like a weaned child with its mother;
>> my soul is like a weaned child that is with me.
>
> O Israel, hope in the LORD
>> from this time on and forevermore.
> (Ps 131)

CHAPTER 3

Howling Winds

A s the days went by, Jeanne kept silent. There is a temptation for strong, proud characters, when surrounded by incomprehension, to fall back stoically onto their own inner resources, to retrench. From their fortress, these men and women look down at the bustle of the world with detachment and maybe with some contempt. But that was not the nature of Jeanne's silence. It was not a challenge. It was suffering, first and foremost.

Her life, built as it was on true inner greatness, enabled her to stand back and look upon what was happening with some detachment, even with humor. This Breton seafarer's daughter knew that "howling winds, rocks, and currents surround the eternal song of the world,"[1] and that they could not impede her. She felt such a strong love welling up inside her. Yet it did not stop her from suffering. To a

---

1. Xavier Grall.

friend who had come to visit her, she said: "Do not call me Jeanne Jugan anymore, but Sister Mary of the Cross." Her friend looked at her. Jeanne was silent. Hers indeed was the silence of Mary at the foot of the cross.

One day, however, Jeanne could contain herself no longer. Coming across Father Le Pailleur, she told him directly: "You have stolen my work. But I give it to you gladly." It had to come out. Now it had been said, probably in a very courteous tone, but also without beating about the bush. Indeed, Jeanne was outspoken. She told things as she saw them, as she felt them. She called a spade a spade, and a theft a theft. It took great strength of character to say things as openly as she did, without in any way losing her calm and good humor.

"... [M]y work ... I give it to you gladly." In those words Jeanne expressed her inner detachment at the same time as her generosity. Yet, however edifying these words may be, there is nonetheless something disturbing about them.

One can only give what is rightfully one's own. Jeanne talked of the work to which she utterly dedicated herself as her personal property. "My work," she said. But did that work truly belong to her? There is no doubt that she poured herself into the work without holding back. Others, however, worked with her. Father Le Pailleur himself was no stranger to the development and success of the work. Indeed, he made a great contribution to it.

Above all, this work was God's work. He is the master of works, the instigator. He is the one who put into Jeanne's heart her charismatic capacity for loving and doing good, her eagerness to run to the aid of the elderly, the poor, and the abandoned. He was the source of the generosity, dynamism, and inner abundance that made Jeanne as strong as she was, even in adversity.

Jeanne probably knew that—but now that "God wanted her for himself, for a work as yet unknown," she needed to know it not just intellectually, but also vitally, experientially. This knowledge must seep into her blood, into her flesh, as well as into her head. She was asked to let herself be totally dispossessed so that she might become that "unknown work," God's work. The inner abundance from which had sprung what she still called "her work" was not rightfully her own. It was God's gift.

"You need to make yourself very little before God," she would often say to postulants and novices among whom she was to live for many years. To one of them she said: "Can you see these workmen carving the white stone for the chapel and how beautiful they are making the stone? You must let yourself be hewn by Our Lord in the same way." Jeanne was speaking from experience. She let herself be hewn by the Master of works. She made herself little in God's hands. We are not born "little" in the sense of the Gospel. We are not born poor at heart. We become such by allowing ourselves to be hewn like the white stone.

When Jeanne walked past a little rose on the grounds, she looked at it. The rose is silent enough to tell the secret of beauty that is beyond any name. But how does the rose become rose? How does it make itself so beautiful? How, without intending to or even realizing it, does it take on the brightness of dawn?

In the yard at the novitiate were wild roses. Jeanne once said to a novice: "You see these rose bushes. They are a little wild. You too are a little wild, but if you let yourself be shaped, you will become a beautiful rose, shaped by God's love. But you must let yourself be humiliated. Instead of turning in on yourself, reach up to God."

The way outlined by Jeanne to this novice for becoming a beautiful rose was also her own. It was the path on which the Lord had set her. She did not turn in or close in on herself, but reached up ever higher. She let herself be carried by the swell of her heart. She did not try to keep for herself that inner fullness like a treasure that was her own. Francis of Assisi would say to his brothers: "Keep nothing for yourself, so that the One who gives himself entirely to you may receive you whole."

Such poverty of heart comes, of course, with a renunciation of ourselves that sometimes causes suffering. At La Tour, Jeanne was more than once rebuffed without much consideration. She was treated like a good girl, if a little simple. Great heart, no doubt, but small head. She was kept out of discussions and decisions regarding the institute, although she was part of the council. Father Le Pailleur ignored her totally. She was denied even the simplest signs of friendship or courtesy. Thus, while the feast days of the "Mothers" and "the Good Father," as Father Le Pailleur was called, were joyfully celebrated, Jeanne was never feted. She was forgotten. She was, after all, only a little woman of no importance.

The fact that she was the foundress and the first of the Little Sisters was carefully kept from the novices. Could such a simple woman be the foundress? The founder, the founding genius, was of course Father Le Pailleur. Everyone knew that, or should know it. Such was the official version. And Jeanne knew it.

Through those years, on the superiors' feast days, the novices organized dramatized presentations evoking the origins of the congregation. Of course these performances followed the official interpretation. A few of the more perspicacious novices noticed how Jeanne was left to herself on those occasions. She was indeed forgotten, and not a word was uttered about her. During these performances she never sat in the front, near the authorities; she stood at the back, unseen. Those novices who suspected she had more of a role later asked her about the origins of the congregation. Jeanne evaded the question, answering simply: "Profit well of your novitiate, be fervent, faithful to our holy rule." Yet she added: "You will never know what it cost."

This veiled revelation said a lot about Jeanne's secret suffering.

We will never know how much Jeanne suffered. One day she made this comment: "You must be like a sack of wool that receives the stone without a sound." Jeanne suffered for years in total silence from the blows she was dealt, before attaining the inalterable peace of an exalted solitude.

Jeanne suffered not only from the incomprehension and dishonesty of those around her, but her suffering also had greater depth. The most sensitive point of her religious being was her intimate relationship with God. Jeanne went through a long, dark night. She knew inner abandonment, enough to lose heart.

She had given herself fully to the work for which God wanted her—and with enthusiasm. She loved that work passionately, as she would have loved her own child, and with the certainty that she was doing the divine will. Then, suddenly, God took it away from her and entrusted it to another, without explanation. She was left alone, set aside, abandoned.

Nothing. A total void. It is a tragic moment when the soul loses itself and no longer knows whom to trust. Had the Lord rejected her, dismissed her?

Jeanne could indeed repeat the psalmist's prayer:

I stretch out my hands to you;
    my soul thirsts for you like a parched land.
Answer me quickly, O LORD;
    my spirit fails.
Do not hide your face from me ...
Teach me the way I should go ...
(Ps 143:6–7, 8)

The Lord's answer is hard to hear. Harder than his silence. "Take your son, your only son Isaac, whom you love, and go to the land of Moriah, and offer him there as a burnt offering..." (Gen 22:2). This order was given to Abraham by God, but every one of God's servants hears it one day. Abraham believed in God's promise to give him descendants. For twenty years, he waited for it to be accomplished. Thus great was his joy when at last Sarah, his wife, already advanced in years, miraculously gave birth to a son! It can be imagined what love he lavished on the child. Suddenly, though, God was asking him to sacrifice this beloved son, the miracle child, his only one, on whom rested the promise of descendants more numerous than the stars of heaven. What a terrible and utterly incomprehensible blow!

Jeanne Jugan was submitted to a comparable test. She too was asked to trust in God with total faith.

Hoping against hope, Abraham obeyed. He believed God would accomplish what he had promised. "He considered the fact that God is able even to raise someone from the dead" (Heb 11:19). He did recover his son and this became a prophetic symbol.

The son who was restored to him, as in a sort of resurrection, was no longer his son only in the flesh. He was, from then on, his son born of faith: the son of faith in the promise on high, born again, the son of a spiritual filiation. Abraham thus became father not only to descendants of the flesh, linked and limited to a clan, to a land, to a particular people. Rather, his paternity took on the dimension of the divine covenant; it opened to the universal, beyond all borders. Abraham saw himself established as "the father of many nations," the father of all those who would share his faith: "[A]nd by your offspring shall all the nations of the earth gain blessing for themselves, because you have obeyed my voice" (Gen 22:18). Descendants "as numerous as the stars of heaven" (Gen 22:17). Abraham's greatness comes from giving up enclosing the covenant and the promises within a dynasty of the flesh, thereby discovering his true lineage as one of faith.

Because of her faith, Jeanne Jugan has her place in that immense posterity of Abraham. She, too, believed. She, too, obeyed. She did not refuse her only one, her child, her work. She gave it with unconditional faith in the All Powerful. In so doing she became God's work herself. What is more, her work was given back to her beyond all expectation.

The Bible reports that King David wanted to build a house for God, a temple worthy of him, that would give shelter to the ark of God. The ark that had accompanied the Israelites' wandering through the desert was still under canvas, while the king now lived a settled and peaceful life in a beautiful cedarwood palace. The time had come to give the ark an honorable place, for the glory of God. Through his prophet Nathan, God let David know: "Are you the one to build me a house to live in? ... I took you from the pasture, from following the sheep ... the LORD declares to you that the LORD will make you a house" (2 Sam 7:5, 8, 11).

This is what Jeanne, too, must know: "I shall make of you my work, my house...."

CHAPTER 4

The Sea

Many men and women call themselves artists, yet express in their work no more than their most superficial inner turmoil. There is nothing authentic or profound; only the froth of life. Too full of themselves, they are unable to produce the inner space of freedom where the Creator Spirit breathes, and to enter the silence where the springs of childhood sing.

Jeanne was silent. Such silence was not a wall in the shade of which she might turn in on herself. It was more of an expanding place of welcome, requiring an ever more attentive, more attuned listening to the calls emanating from nature, from humans, and from God. In truth, it was an opening of the whole being to the breath of the Creator. Beyond all her inner tensions, Jeanne recovered the freshness and malleability she had had as a child, when she was pure receptiveness, like soft wax in the hands of an artist.

Jeanne was born in Cancale, a small fishing port in the north of Brittany. Growing up in the modest home of a family of fishermen, she was not yet four year old when her father was lost at sea. In order to feed her four children, Jeanne's mother did menial work. The family owned a small herd of cattle, and Jeanne was still very young when she started looking after the cows on the hills above the bay of Mont-Saint-Michel. Her days were spent in solitude and silence, facing the immensity of the sea, the mysterious sea whence her father had not returned. That sea nevertheless held a fascination for her, limitless blue in the sun, as far as the eye could see; a sea that could be dark and frightening when, under a low gray sky, wild winds chased howling waves, like terrified beasts, into the rocky cliffs of the Pointe du Grouin.

The sight of the high sea, whether calm or tormented, opened the child's soul to vast horizons, to limitless spaces. There was nothing there to stop the eye gazing into infinity: no barriers, no successive planes, no structured landscape. Unhindered, endless sea met endless sky along the horizon. No port of call, no rock to scale. Blue on blue or gray on gray, sea and sky merged into each other and became one. All at once the soul was engulfed in immensity. At such times Jeanne must have felt very small and yet so big!

As evening fell, Jeanne returned home. The house was small, a fisherman's cottage with a thatched roof and beaten-earth floor. The family gathered in the only room. A fire was lit in the hearth, a candle on the table. When bedtime came, her mother would gather the children around her, put her hands together, and shut her eyes in prayer. Little

Jeanne gazed in awe at her mother's face, turned inward and open to the invisible. Thus she learned that there were inner spaces, areas of light, vaster still than the bay of Le Mont-Saint-Michel, and so bright you had to close your eyes in order to see them.

Years later, in the alleys at La Tour, by the ponds or in her room, alone and silent before God, Jeanne rediscovered the soul of her childhood—so small, yet so great. She opened herself to the wind from the high seas. She let herself be carried ever higher by the swell of her heart. Her silence was a growing of her whole being. A proverb from Zaire says: "A single tree makes much noise as it falls, but no one hears the growing of the forest."

The worshipping heart frees itself of all its strictures, of all its self-centeredness. The inner space it offers to God becomes ever greater, ever deeper. Thus Jeanne, without even realizing it, opened herself ever wider to God's great purpose. She joined "Yahweh's Poor," those "worshippers unknown to the world and to the prophets themselves"[1]; this "people humble and lowly ... [who] shall seek refuge in the name of the LORD" (Zeph 3:12). Throughout history, through vicissitudes and persecutions, this "small remnant" never ceased on their journey. Unrecognized and despised by those in high places, they carry within the poverty of their hearts the radiance of the one God.

Like Saint Francis of Assisi, and following in the steps of many others, Jeanne takes her place among those men and women who do not seek to be ranked first and do not push themselves to the front of the world stage. These unknown

---

1. Blaise Pascal, *Pensées*, part 12, no. 788.

worshippers know themselves to be small and frail, even sinners. Yet in their distress they are open to a visitation from above. In vessels of clay they carry a ray of glory. Their precious treasure nestles at the heart of their poverty and frailty. In their poverty their hearts grow in proportion to this infinite treasure.

The kingdom of God will always be hidden in this world. But Yahweh's poor can see its advent in the humblest and frailest of beings. What could be more humble, or more frail, than a little child? "For a child has been born for us, a son given to us …": this prophecy of Isaiah is still true. It encompasses the secret of the world. It casts its light on the whole of history. Those who walk in darkness, those who limp in the shadows, see the rising of a light, and that light shines in the eyes of a little child. Wondrous paradox: a small being who cannot yet talk is himself the Word in its fullness. The light in his eyes is as splendid as the dawn.

> Jesus without wealth or any outward show of knowledge has his own order of holiness. He made no discoveries; he did not reign, but he was humble, patient, thrice holy to God, terrible to devils, and without sin. With what great pomp and marvelously magnificent array he came in the eyes of the heart, which perceive wisdom![2]

2. Pascal, *Pensées*, translated with an Introduction by A. J. Krailsheimer (Harmondsworth, UK: Penguin Classics, 1981) [Translator's note].

Seaside landscape of Cancale on the northern coast of Brittany, France.

The house in Cancale where Jeanne Jugan was born.

Interior of the house where Jeanne was born.

Ferme Les Grands Pres, where Jeanne's parents worked as day laborers.

La Mettrie-aux-Chouettes, the house where Jeanne worked as a kitchen maid for the Viscountess de la Choue.

The apartment at Saint-Servan where Jeanne took in the first elderly, infirm woman in 1839.

The kitchen of the Saint-Servan apartment; the ladder leads to Jeanne's attic bedroom.

Saint-Servan's apartment attic where Jeanne and her companions prayed at night.

The dining room of the House of the Cross where Jeanne and her companions moved in 1842.

The house in Rennes opened in 1846.

A small room in the house at Dinan where it is believed that Jeanne Jugan, with the help of Father Felix Mossot of the Brothers of Saint John of God, drafted the first Rule of Life of the Little Sisters.

*Chapel at Rennes as it
appears today.*

Interior of the house at Rennes.

The novitiate building at La Tour where Jeanne spent her last years in the room just above the main door.

The old sewing room at La Tour where Jeanne spent her days with the novices.

La Tour chapel, the balcony where Jeanne prayed when she was aged and infirm.

The chapel at La Tour as is appears today.

The room in which Jeanne died in 1879.

Crypt at La Tour where Jeanne is buried.

*Detail from the painting for the beatification of Jeanne Jugan
by the Italian artist Dina Belotti.*

CHAPTER 5

Divine Dawn

DESPITE THE MONOTONY OF DAYS, life at La Tour presented changing aspects from season to season, and it sometimes took on a picturesque appearance. In the harvest season, for example, the Little Sisters harvesting hay were truly a sight to behold. A ballet of frolicking novices provided highly colorful entertainment, much enjoyed by the local children. The Sisters wore scarves of many colors, inspiring the imagination of the children who watched them. Or they might wear all manner of straw hats, at which they were the first to laugh.

Jeanne Jugan's daily walks across the estate were also sometimes enlivened by unexpected minor events. On one occasion she surprised some young prowlers. One of them, grown up, told the tale with touches of humor:

> It was springtime ... I was with the two Petel brothers—
> François, about ten years old, and Louis, who was
> younger. They took me along with them; I was four. At

that time, there was no wall at La Morinais (a patch of land that lay next to the La Tour estate), only a quickset hedge, through which you could see the strawberries very well. Such beautiful strawberries ripening in the sun! Just the sight of them was mouthwatering. The two brothers made a hole in the hedge and went in; being the smallest, I had no difficulty slipping in after them. There was no one there. No sisters. We helped ourselves to strawberries. It was a heavenly moment. But all of a sudden I saw François running off as fast as he could: Jeanne Jugan was walking toward us, threatening us with her long stick. I can still picture her: tall, very tall, thin, bony, with an austere face. Appropriate in the circumstances, since she was not coming to congratulate us. The two brothers had run away faster than I had, and with my short legs, I fell behind. I can still see Jeanne just next to me saying: "You little thief!" And yet, she didn't frighten me. I went back through the hedge, not quite as easily as I had gone in....

No, Jeanne and her stick were not frightening. She was not the terrifying angel with burning sword chasing Adam and Eve out of earthly paradise. "Her stick, in the eyes of a budding thief, was only a common stick, like the ones you find in a bundle of firewood...."

There was once a more alarming encounter, which could have had a tragic outcome. Several Little Sisters were walking in the novitiate garden saying the rosary. Jeanne was among them. Suddenly the workmen were heard shouting: "Run! Run! Get out of the way!" A raging bull had stampeded out of the cattle shed, wrecking everything in its path, and was heading straight for the Little Sisters. There was a moment of panic. "Lie down, little ones!" shouted Jeanne. She, meanwhile, stood her ground and faced the beast, lifting her small stick: "Stop, I command you." As if startled by such calm, the beast stopped in its tracks and allowed itself to be led back. It is easy to be reminded here of Francis of Assisi taming the terrible wolf of Gubbio. The story of Jeanne's life at La Tour is adorned with many *fioretti*. Yet these picturesque and sometimes wonderful happenings were still only external events. The true miracle was happening inside. This was her inner transformation and growth—quite literally, a new birth.

The year was 1864. After a very hot summer, autumn had come with its red and gold foliage, and also with its storms. The pheasants that only the day before had run through the sunlit stubble fields had vanished. The leaves had been falling, and gusting winds were blowing off the last ones. The trees, now stripped, had lost their pride; bare, they offered themselves up to the light, the spaces among their branches filled with sky. The paths and the undergrowth were strewn with leaves as luminous as vermeil. At certain times of day, under a gray sky, light seemed to rise from the ground. It was not the flame of summer, but a discreet, soft light, tinted with pink, like the light of dawn.

Jeanne loved to walk along those quiet footpaths. Rosary in hand, she would let herself be suffused by silence. She prayed and meditated as she walked. For some time now, a word of Scripture had been holding her attention: "the one who is righteous will live by faith" (Gal 3:11; see also Rom 1:17). She shared this word with a young sister preparing for her profession, confiding that it was foremost in her thoughts.

A lifetime may not suffice to truly understand the meaning of this word. We only know well what we experience for ourselves. At this time Jeanne was entering deep into the truth of that message. In personalities that are rich in inner resources, it always takes a long time for poverty to make its way to the core of being.

Indeed, it is only when all our human assurances and sources of support are taken away, and when we find ourselves in an utter void, that we can enter into the full light of the word: "The upright will live through faith."

Then rises the cry of the poor: "Without you, I am lost." All that remains is God and his word of love. The upright live by that word, through pure, bare faith. Henceforth, only faith justifies their existence, in the full sense of the term. "Without you, I am lost. But with you, I exist; I exist through your word. For your word is a word of love." That word is not founded on my merit, on my works, however holy they may be. It is connected to nothing. It comes first. It always comes first. It is the foundation of everything. It is in the beginning. It is my beginning. When I hear it, it is for me a new birth. Flesh is not all that is needed for someone to be born. Also needed is a word: a word of love. "Through your word I am born, your word makes me live. Here I am living with you. And all my existence with you is justified."

Carried by that faith, Jeanne entered Advent, that liturgical period during which the Church relives the waiting and expectation of God's people, in the spirit of the prophets. Her whole being was open to that hope, "earth calling out to a new world." Then came the beauty of the feast of Christmas. As it was every year, the Nativity was celebrated at La Tour with fervor and joy.

On the afternoon of Christmas Day 1864, Jeanne, her soul filled with the gentleness of this great mystery, strolled the grounds in the usual way, listening in her heart to the echo of the word from the Office of the day: "Today I have begotten you, you are my beloved Child...."

On her way she came across a group of young postulants. Immediately the young women, who were fond of her, formed a circle around her, as if to stop her from walking away. Then Jeanne let her inner joy burst forth. She started singing with them the familiar Christmas carol:

Il est né, le divin Enfant.
Jouez, hautbois, résonnez, musettes.
Il est né, le divin Enfant,
Chantons tous son avènement ... [1]

Jeanne's face was radiant. She was laughing, the clear laugh of a child. On this Feast of Christmas, Jeanne had become a child with the Child. The divine Child had been born in the poverty of her heart, and she was singing her joy with the young sisters she had just met on her way. Then she resumed her walk, singing on simply, joyously, waving her stick through the air, as if beating time.

The Child was born, but in the night, as in Bethlehem, God reveals himself in the heart of our darkness. His coming does not dispel the night; it transfigures it. Our wish is to encounter God in full light. Yet the experience of mystics shows that while the night is still there, when suffused by the Child's humble light, it becomes a light-filled shadow. The mystery of Christmas in the hearts of saints is of the same essence as this dark light. The light pervades the

---

1. "Born on earth the divine Christ Child, / Oboes, rejoice, with bagpipes vying; / Born on earth the divine Christ Child, / Sing to welcome the Savior mild ... " English words by Jacqueline Froom, © Oxford University Press, 1967. Reproduced by permission (Translator's note).

night, secretly, humbly. It does not dissipate the darkness; it appeases it, tames it, and makes its dwelling in it.

In a seventeenth-century painting by the master Georges de La Tour, *The New-born Child*, two women gaze in silence at a baby. The mother, viewed face on, holds the swaddled child in her arms. The other woman, viewed in profile, guards with her hand the flame of a candle she is holding. The blackness of night is the only backdrop. Night and silence. There is no decor, no furniture. Nothing that might distract the eye. No evident religious sign. Yet the whole mystery is contained in that recollection in the night. Only the humble candle, the flame of which is not even visible, projects its light over the sleeping child, who becomes the illuminated focus of the scene. The shadow is still there, but peaceful now, and filled with the light that emanates from the child.

The same night light is present in *The Adoration of the Shepherds* by the same painter. The flame of a candle, half hidden by the hand that guards it, brings out of the gloom some shepherds huddled around the manger where the newborn child lies. The faces are rough, the gestures every-day ones: one shepherd removes his hat, another leans on his staff, holding it in his gnarled hand; a woman brings a bowl. A primitive, crude world, still steeped in shadow, is revealed and transfigured by the humble light radiating from the Child. Faces are just beginning to relax, smiles to appear; a lamb stretches its muzzle toward the Child as if to kiss him. The night winds have abated. The serene part of darkness now reigns: a light-filled shadow, imbued with God's tenderness.

Such is the mystery of Christmas in the hearts of saints. Far from dissipating all darkness, the Child's light becomes integrated into it, hollows it out, and in it makes its refuge, its dwelling, its sanctuary. It is a light in the night, as humble and deep as the mystery it reveals.

CHAPTER 6

The Moment of Truth

FROM THE BEGINNING, THE IDEAL of the Little Sisters of the Poor had been to live in poverty with the poor, relying only on the generosity of benefactors—in other words, living on what they collected. Such an ideal meant day-to-day insecurity, and it required total trust, lived a day at a time.

Jeanne Jugan had given a shining example of that trust in God who would not forget his poor. She had shown the way by her example. An English tourist who visited her when she was in full activity, at the time of the founding of the house at Dinan, was struck by the trust shown by Jeanne. He did not failed to remark on it: "She did not know," he wrote, "whence provisions for the next day would come, but persevered, firmly convinced that God would never abandon the poor."

On occasion the Little Sisters accepted fixed sources of income or endowments, but those were an exception. Collecting remained the rule, and it had not been felt necessary to spell things out or lay down the law in this matter.

But fifteen years later, the congregation was better known and was being offered more and more legacies. These represented guaranteed means of support. All that was required was to convert the money into interest-bearing investments. Doing so would secure the future of the houses and their guests.

The path was easy, and very tempting, but was it the right one? In 1865, the gift of an annuity of 4,000 francs, with the congregation as beneficiary, provided the opportunity to raise the question.

A lay friend, the Comte de Bertou, who helped the Little Sisters with the financial management of their houses, felt moved in the circumstances to draw their attention to an important point:

> If you will allow me to give my humble opinion, you must accept it (this legacy) only on condition that you are authorized to forgo the interest so that the capital may serve towards payment for your (Paris) house. You should own only the buildings in which you live and, for the rest, live on daily charity. If the Little Sisters were known to have investments, they would lose the right to the charity that kept the Israelites alive in the desert, and should they store manna, it would start rotting in their hands, as once happened to God's people.

His remarks had the great merit of confronting the Little Sisters with their responsibilities. They must make a choice, and their decision would affect the future of the congregation. Truly, the very charism of the Little Sisters was in the balance.

The situation could not have been stated more clearly, and the final reference to the experience of the People of God in the desert was in itself enlightening. Not a mere literary figure, it had deep meaning.

The comparison with the biblical experience threw a bright light onto the Little Sisters' charism by rooting it in the history of the People of God. This charism was suddenly shown to be the same as that which marked the founding experience of the People of the Covenant: total faith and trust lived day by day, down to the material aspects of life. One could live by this charism only by holding oneself in the condition of the Exodus, of the walk in the desert toward the Promised Land. The only God, the God of the Covenant, lets himself be known only by those who are resolutely committed to this experience of faith and trust. The only God, the God of the Covenant, will always be the One who is utterly trusted.

In truth, the friendly voice that advised the Little Sisters in this decisive hour came from afar and carried a long way. It had a prophetic tone, which took on its full meaning in view of a world that, in the second half of the nineteenth century, was increasingly becoming a world of money. With the advent of industrial society and big investors came the hitherto unknown prominence of banks. "The stock exchange became to that generation what cathedrals had been to the Middle Ages."[1] Money, the symbol of

---

1. Alexandre Dumas fils.

security, was placed in banks where it could bear fruit. It meant a secure future. The Little Sisters' charism—that of trust in the Lord lived day by day, in close solidarity with the poor—was in opposition to that world. Making a choice was imperative.

If the Comte de Bertou's comments alerted the Little Sisters to the seriousness of their decision, it nonetheless left them pondering which choice to make. Indeed, for their own part, benefactors who wanted to give them an income put pressure on them to accept, on the strength of the good cause they were serving. Should they not above all secure the future of their houses? On the congregation council, opinions were divided. A final decision was put off as the Little Sisters consulted several bishops, to no avail—they could not see things any more clearly.

At that point one of the sisters, a member of the council, was bold enough to suggest: "What if we asked Sister Mary of the Cross (Jeanne Jugan) what she thinks?" How was the suggestion received within the council? How did Father Le Pailleur react? No one knows, because all documents referring to Father Le Pailleur's activities or opinions were destroyed between 1882 and 1900. The fact remains that in the end, in desperation, it was decided to call upon Jeanne Jugan. She was summoned to the council.

Thus at the very moment when the congregation was setting off on the path to security, with the help of human support, we see emerging from the shadows Jeanne, the first of the Little Sisters, the one whom "God had set apart for his own work" but who had been cast aside. All human support had been withdrawn from her. She had put herself in God's hands for her crossing of the desert. She was living this experience of poverty trusting in the God of the Covenant. She truly was the one "coming up from the desert, leaning upon her lover" (Sg 8:5, *NAB*). Now all eyes were on her. Did she not embody the founding charism? Was she not that living charism?

Calling upon Jeanne in such circumstances was an implicit recognition of her position as foundress. It was treating her as the repository of the founding charism, as the one who was at its source and who could bear witness to it with the most truth and authenticity.

One can easily imagine Jeanne's surprise at being summoned to the council, when she had been forgotten for years and was now living in silence and adoration, having handed over to God anything that concerned the future of the congregation. That future was no longer her own business, but God's. She had let go of it completely.

Anyone else, at such a time, might have triumphed secretly and made others understand that she was "indispensable." That was not Jeanne's reaction. On the contrary, she said: "I am only a poor ignorant woman. What can I say?" This was not feigned humility; she truly believed it. She reckoned she had nothing more to say. But as others insisted, she agreed: "Since you so wish, I shall obey."

So she attended the council and expressed her opinion clearly: the order should carry on receiving no fixed income and trusting completely in God. She had not the slightest hesitation. The trail was marked out; all they had to do was follow it. Her option prevailed. A circular was sent to the various houses, outlining the appropriate conduct in future: the congregation would not be permitted to own any investments, any permanent fixed income....

Jeanne placed her signature on the official act, after those of other council members. A humble signature at the foot of the page, the only one without flourish or embellishment. A firm signature, but austere, without the least trace of triumphalism. It will be noted that Father Le Pailleur's signature does not appear on this item.

At the end of the council meeting, Jeanne returned to the novitiate as if nothing had happened. No one asked her to stay at the motherhouse. The interlude over, Jeanne returned to solitude, silence, and oblivion. She was once again alone with God, simple and silent as growing wheat or a flowering rose.

CHAPTER 7

True Foundations

THROUGHOUT THOSE LONG YEARS OF solitude at La Tour, Jeanne's outlook on people and things was constantly being purified and deepened. Little by little, it was moving closer to God's merciful outlook on the world.

By putting her whole being and destiny into God's hands, Jeanne was freeing herself from focusing tightly on herself and was opening herself up to closer communion with the world near and far. She was getting the measure of the great creative and redemptive design. It was said of Saint Francis of Assisi that "the moment he renounced everything he was also breaking down all the barriers which separated him from the creative act," and that "everything that was taken away from him broadened his horizon."[1] That same opening up can be observed in Jeanne.

---

1. Louis Lavelle.

Many events were taking place in the world during those years. Some were especially tragic: the 1870 Franco-German war, the siege of Paris, the Commune. There were also the First Vatican Council, prematurely interrupted by war, and the capture of Rome by Garibaldi's troops... All these events found an echo at La Tour and a place in Jeanne's huge heart. The Little Sister of the Poor brought to God all the woes of the world. She would very much have wanted to take out into this tormented world her peace and her joy.

"She taught us," related a sister who was a novice at the time, "how our prayers must be universal, especially in time of war. She started (her rosary) with the great intentions of the holy Church, our dear religious family, through to the smallest details of those who were suffering and needed help from God...."

If, in her solitude, Jeanne was communing with the life of the world, she paid particular attention to the small world around her. She had understood quickly that, although she could not expend her energies on the outside, her current situation was showing her another way. Her mission was not over. She had no official responsibility, but her life among the postulants and novices allowed her to play an important, if discreet, role in their training. Was not her mission, from now on, precisely to help all these young women to develop their vocation, by revealing to them through her presence and her own life the charism specific to the Little Sisters? Jeanne inadvertently found herself in a unique, ideal situation to communicate to postulants and novices the true spirit of the congregation.

In moving Jeanne away from the management of the institute, in sidelining her from the community in the motherhouse and relegating her to life among the novices, Father Le Pailleur was unaware that he was handing over to her privileged territory on which to play her true role as foundress in the best possible conditions, in the deepest possible way. True foundations are hidden; they lie deep in the ground.

Through her charisma, Jeanne would influence many young postulants and novices (whose numbers would reach into the hundreds); she would thus ensure the spiritual future of the congregation. The mystery of Christ remains true:

> The stone that the builders rejected
>> has become the chief cornerstone.
> This is the LORD's doing...
> (Ps 118:22–23)

So Jeanne lived in the midst of the young, sharing the same building. She had no specific responsibilities, but took part in their lives. She was present above all through the attention she gave them. Simple and welcoming, she was easily approachable. Everyone who addressed her was won over by the gentle smile that transfigured her face when she was spoken to. "She looked so kindly," says one of the young women, "she appeared so affable, so simple, that one was drawn to her."

"She was a lovely little mother who loved us very much," reports another. And because she loved them, she could also sometimes be demanding when it came to their training.

In the mornings, novices saw her participate in the Mass with great fervor. For Jeanne, it was a meaningful moment, a true encounter with the Lord, deep and direct communion with his sacrifice, with the gift of his life for the world.

During the day, aside from time spent in chapel before the Blessed Sacrament, she was most often to be found in the sewing room, knitting woolen stockings. As she grew older, her eyes tired more quickly and she could no longer apply herself for long. At recreation time she was the life and soul of the group. Her cheerfulness was infectious. She liked to laugh and make others laugh. In the summer, for instance, when she went out on a walk with the novices and handed out straw hats, she would keep the funniest, shabbiest one for herself. It amused the young ones. In her daily comings and goings, when she passed a group of novices, she never failed to greet them with a friendly word.

It was precisely through those informal meetings that Jeanne imparted to the young ones the spirit that inhabited her. She did it in all spontaneity, without forethought. It was as if rays of light sprang out and drew strength from the very quality of their relationship. To the novices she felt so close, so loving, that she became the living image of the spirit she meant to pass on to them.

In trying to pin down and define that spirit, one theme comes up again and again in Jeanne's recommendations to the novices: "Be little, make yourselves very little," she would tell them. It was a kind of refrain. Indeed, she was convinced that to be close to the humblest and least, you had to become very little yourself. You cannot establish truly close links while keeping your distance or placing yourself above others. The most high Son of God himself became the humblest of men in order to be close to all.

Jeanne gave great importance to this closeness. You had to be little in order to be close to the least. Such was the vocation, the charism of the Little Sisters of the Poor. It was for them not just a matter of giving shelter and food to the abandoned elderly. They were also to bring them a certain quality of relationship, a presence, a closeness that would draw these people out of their isolation and free them from their anguish. The Little Sisters were not to be ladies who condescend to devote some time daily to looking after poor people. No, they must become little themselves as they entered a close relationship with the humblest and most forsaken. We are not naturally "little," in the evangelical sense. We become so. It takes time and much renunciation. Above all, we must ask for it as a grace. Such is the way Jeanne prepared the young novices for their mission, by making them aware of a fundamental demand of their vocation.

There was another point on which Jeanne insisted, connected to the first and complementary. It is not easy to define. In her, it was a flame, first and foremost. Her eyes lit up when she spoke of it. Others could feel the fire of passion rising up in her. One day she pronounced these burning words, magnificent in their simplicity: "What happiness for us, to be a Little Sister of the Poor! Making the poor happy is everything...." The whole mission and happiness of the Little Sisters is contained here: making the poor happy, giving happiness to the poor.

Jeanne's message to the novices can be summed up in these two elements: be little in order to be close to the most humble, and be close to make them happy. There can be no better definition of the founding charism of the Little Sisters of the Poor.

Making the poor happy is no easy thing, and Jeanne knew it. We can give them shelter, feed, clothe, and care for them, without making them happy. Most elderly people have been marked by life. They carry a heavy burden in their bodies and in their infirmities, but also in their souls, often wounded by painful experiences such as separation, bereavement, loneliness, and, sometimes, rejection. Some of them are raw, as if flayed alive.

"Old age is like a shipwreck," in the words of Charles de Gaulle. A person tries to salvage what is left of a little world, but nothing new appears on the horizon. No new day dawns; no new light comes to illuminate existence. There is nothing to expect from life other than increasing loneliness. The loneliness of the elderly! Do we really know what it is? One of them said: "The deep pain of the poor is that no one needs our friendship."

In Jean Giono's novel, *Que ma joie demeure* (May My Joy Remain), one of the characters describes the men he saw at an inn, seated at table around him: "The eyes of each one were haunted by the same anxiety. More than anxiety, fear. More than fear, blankness. A place where there was no anxiety, or fear anymore; oxen under the yoke."

Jesus may have been moved by a similar sight as he watched the crowds coming toward him like sheep without a shepherd, joyless, nameless, aimless creatures. Filled with pity, he exclaimed; "Come to me, all you that are weary and are carrying heavy burdens, and I will give you rest..." (Mt 11:28). These words of Jesus were the expression of

God's merciful gaze on his people. A gaze not of mere compassion, but rather of resurrection. A gaze that restores to life and greatness. A gaze that grants each one a name. A loving gaze. Jesus said, "[The shepherd] calls his own sheep by name..." (Jn 10:3).

This is what "making the poor happy" means: rescuing them from their anonymous solitude, giving back to them a name and face, prompting them to be open to a new awareness of themselves and their dignity. To do all that, we must love them. A poor person is not happy just because he is given shelter, fed, and cared for, but also—and most importantly—because he feels loved and given consideration. Without that quality of relationship, a home for the elderly can be a sad place, so sad it may kill.

Consideration is what we bestow least and with the greatest difficulty. We easily give of our money, time, or knowledge. We more rarely bestow our consideration. When we show someone esteem, we acknowledge that they bring us something, and we therefore place them on an equal footing with and sometimes even above ourselves, whereas in giving our money, time, or knowledge, we might place ourselves above them and immediately put them in our debt.

"Making the poor happy," for Jeanne, meant granting them the quality of gaze and attention that would make them aware of their dignity, of their greatness as sons and daughters of God.

Some may be surprised, on reading various accounts by the Little Sisters who were novices at the time, by the importance Jeanne gave to silence. She asked the novices not to close doors too noisily, nor to storm down the stairs. This was her way of teaching them to respect others; she had in mind the elderly or the sick who would later be entrusted to their care.

One day a novice was doing the housework in the room above Jeanne's bedroom. She was going at it heartily, and the noise could be heard all around, not unlike a cavalry charge! Jeanne asked for the young sister to come and see her. "My little one," she said to her, "when you do the housework, especially around the sick, you must take great care not to make a noise, to handle objects gently, and not to strike the floor with your heels when you walk.... It is very tiring for the sick. You must be silent!"

"The elderly," she also said, "are sensitive to small attentions. And it is a way of winning them over to God." Evidently Jeanne did not lose sight of the religious dimension. However, for her this concern, too, was governed by respect and discretion. When it came to prayer formulas, "she often stressed," confided a novice, "that we should later on be careful not to use too many devotional prayers: 'You will weary your old people,' she would say. 'They will get bored, and wander off for a smoke ... even during the rosary!'"

It was through such lessons that Jeanne awakened the novices' spirits to respect for others and showed them how they could work at making poor people happy. She so wanted to communicate to them her great love for the poor and the elderly!

Jeanne herself had that quality of gaze and attention for the novices and the postulants. She was attentive to their sorrows, to their joys, to the life of each one. It was, incidentally, the best way to awaken them to their mission as Little Sisters of the Poor.

The young women were very willing to confide in her. "I was going through a difficult time," testified one of them. "I was struggling and could not overcome the problem! Then I came across her and she asked me to help her go up the stairs. I asked her to say an Ave Maria for me. She replied: 'Yes, my little one.' And immediately my great sorrow disappeared." All Jeanne had said was: "Yes, my little one." Those simple words were enough because they revealed to the young sister that she was no longer alone in her sorrow, that Jeanne was sharing it and that she was holding her in prayer. Those very simple, eminently discreet words opened a window onto the gentle nearness of God.

However, there were not only happy times at La Tour. There were also dark days, days of grief. The year 1857 was particularly grueling for the novices. Five of their number died that year. What indescribable sadness on that autumn day when, for the fifth time, the bell tolled over La Tour! It was a dull, sad day. Even the countryside, drowned in fog, seemed to be weeping. The procession of Little Sisters made its slow way down the path to the cemetery, behind the coffin of the young sister, the fifth to have been taken away that autumn by typhoid fever. It was as though a curse hung heavy over La Tour. Two ponds, thought to be responsible for the illness, had been drained. When would it ever end?

The repeated deaths of novices were a trial for all the sisters. They were felt even more painfully by Jeanne. She was so close to the young ones. She knew them all and loved them as a mother.

Far from becoming discouraged, Jeanne thought only of helping the novices to overcome their sorrow and to see in their trial a way to stronger faith and higher hope. It was also for her the chance to open their hearts to the pain of the world. Throughout their lives, the Little Sisters would have to be alongside much suffering and bereavement. They would have to share the sorrows of the poor. Such was the way in which Jeanne was preparing them for their mission and, in her solitude, fulfilling her own mission as foundress.

CHAPTER 8

The Gold of Sunset

IT IS NOT ENOUGH TO SAY yes once. Nor even for a year, or ten, or twenty. You have to say it throughout your life, to the end and in spite of everything. Day after day. On foggy days as well as sunny ones; in illness as in full health.

Many of the saints we venerate died young. They did not know old age, the weariness of time, the trials of great age, with its heaviness, its infirmities, its dependence, its long nights of insomnia, solitude, and sometimes anguish.

Jeanne spoke little about her health, but in 1873 she fell ill and was confined to bed for several weeks. She recovered, but without regaining full vigor. She was eighty-one years old. From then on, a novice would accompany her on her walks. She still walked with a firm step, one hand resting on the young Little Sister's shoulder.

Yet as days went by, her movements became more and more difficult. She rarely left the infirmary. She was still lucid and present. Being nearly blind, she could no longer read or sew. She spent her time praying and meditating, her rosary in her hand. Her waxen, diaphanous face seemed at first strikingly thin. But the moment someone spoke to her, her features relaxed and lit up. Her smile was beautiful.

This serenity came from the depths of her being. More than ever, Jeanne lived by her faith. What reassured her before God was not the work to which she had given herself and which was now developing beyond all expectation without her. That work, she knew, was not her own. It was God's work. Jeanne had delivered all of it into God's hands. In truth, what reassured her before God and gave her total trust, a child's trust, was knowing herself to be very little and very poor. Yes, God was, and that was enough. One day, she had confided in a novice: "When you are old, you will no longer see anything. As for me, I no longer see anything but God ... He sees me, that is enough."

Spoken toward the close of a long life of dispossession, those simple words have the density and brilliance of gold. They are the gold of sunset. Some sunsets are brighter, more triumphant, than the dawn.

Let us enter the large room of the infirmary. Evening has come, the end of a day and of a life. Jeanne, seated, is silent. She is meditating. The sculptor Aimé-Jules Dalou (1838–1902) represented her wearing her great cape, her head covered by a hood. Only her face is visible, with its fine, relaxed features. The eyes are lowered; the right hand, resting on her knee, opens a little as if to receive the invisible. This is no longer Jeanne the collector of bread, who traveled tirelessly on every road in all types of weather, her large basket on her arm. This is Jeanne, beggar for God, humble and trusting, tranquil and serene. Jeanne is praying; she makes herself very little; she loses herself in God, in an attitude of calm and adoration. She appears to be enveloped in the great mantle of God's mercy.

It is the peace of evening, the evening of life. Jeanne sometimes remembers the little rose on the grounds. She can no longer see it, but she has contemplated it so much that the little rose has finally flowered within her.

At La Tour, when they saw her serenity, the novices realized something forceful and luminous was happening within her. They loved her, and secretly venerated her. For them, she was like the evening sun that spreads its light in profusion as it goes down.

Some days, Jeanne appeared at the infirmary window and, smiling, waved to the novices gathered in the yard. The young ones responded by waving their arms and sometimes with cheerful jostling. Jeanne was happy. She was getting through, they were in perfect communion. Future and past held hands in shared youthfulness of heart and spirit. The novices exulted and clapped their hands. They were the mountain stream that, bouncing along, acclaimed its source. Then, radiant, Jeanne called out her ultimate message: "Be very little ... only the little ones are pleasing to God."

The serenity and joy that increasingly flooded Jeanne's heart left room only for praise. Everything became cause for praise. The small events of the day, or the memory of what she had once contemplated during her walks on the grounds and the countryside: the flowers, the light, the fields, the woods—everything echoed in her with a song of praise to God.

One winter morning, she awoke to discover from the window of her room that snow had fallen during the night and covered buildings, trees, and yard with its immaculate whiteness. "Look," she exclaimed in wonder, "it's so beautiful!" And she added: "My Bridegroom did this." Jeanne lived at the heart of the covenant. Everything beautiful was in her eyes the work of the One she loved and who loved her. None had understood better than she this word of the prophet Isaiah to the people of the covenant: "For your Maker is your husband" (Isa 54:5). Jeanne was living this daily, in all simplicity: the covenant as a bond of love, as feast of the heart, with the whole of creation.

Jeanne summed up this praise that rose from her heart in a simple formula she repeated ceaselessly: "God be praised and blessed in his creatures." It was her "canticle of the creatures," her song of the world in the evening light. The long silence of a whole life was flowering into endless praise. Jeanne was going to God with the whole of creation.

In her song, she also enveloped everything that was being done around her, all the work of the superiors and the Little Sisters. There was not a shadow of resentment in her. Her heart was overflowing with gratitude to God for all the great and beautiful things that were being accomplished. She lifted up her hands to the heavens when she saw the host of novices. The numerous vocations were in her eyes the most beautiful sign of divine blessing on the work undertaken.

When one or other of her friends from the first little community of Saint-Servan came to visit her, Jeanne instinctively straightened her tall, frail frame, and, filled with enthusiasm, she showed them the various realizations: the large, brand-new church, the tower with the statue of Saint Joseph at the top, the spacious buildings, and, above all, the many postulants and novices, in whose hearts God had placed the same love for the poor as lived in her own. For all those blessings, Jeanne was unceasing in her praise. She was singing her *Magnificat*.

In July 1878, one year before her death, the general chapter of the congregation was held at La Tour. It gathered 130 capitular sisters representing the 170 houses that formed the institute at that time. A meeting of the chapter is always an important time in the life of a congregation. Orientations are chosen and decisions made for the future. The most solemn moment of all is the election of the superior general, charged with implementing these orientations and decisions.

That solemn moment had come. Outside the door of the great hall where the election was taking place stood the group of novices especially trained in Gregorian chant. They were waiting for the door to open, ready to enter and sing the *Te Deum* in thanksgiving for the election that would give the congregation a new superior general.

They were kept waiting in awesome silence. Then something unexpected happened. Led and supported by one of the sisters came Jeanne herself. She was all smiles, and appeared amused to be there too, outside the door of the chapter, awaiting developments. She exchanged a few pleasantries with the novices, which broke the ice and introduced a touch of simplicity into the solemnity of the moment. As one of the novices expressed surprise at seeing her there, outside the door, Jeanne said with humor: "Yes, here am I, waiting with you ... yet I should be inside!"

This comment was made without a hint of bitterness. Jeanne was simply calling to mind, without dwelling on it, the comical and somewhat surreal aspect of the situation: the foundress, the first Little Sister, aged eighty-six, was waiting like the least of the novices at the door of the chapter that was deciding on the future of the congregation; she, too, was waiting for the door to open so she could sing the *Te Deum*. Jeanne laughed it off, without attempting to explain the situation to the young ones. She was now far above, like a lark in the sky, and looked down on the earth where she had suffered so much. Nothing could now disturb the peace in her heart. She was free. And she was waiting for another door to open, ready to sing another *Te Deum*.

Before she went through that ultimate door, she was granted a great joy. On March 1, 1879, Pope Leo XIII approved the constitutions of the Little Sisters for a period of seven years. The congregation then numbered 2,400 members. Jeanne's joy was complete, and she continued in ceaseless thanksgiving.

When summer came, Jeanne was clearly weakening. On August 27, she made her confession for the last time. The next morning, after Mass, she took ill. She was put to bed. After regaining consciousness, she received the sacrament of Anointing of the Sick. She was praying softly: "Eternal Father, open your door today to the most wretched of your daughters." She added: "O Mary, my dear Mother, come to me; you know I love you and how I long to see you." Those were her last words. She passed away peacefully.

The door had opened wide before her. This was not the door of the council of the congregation or of the general chapter. It was the door of the kingdom of light and peace promised to the little ones and the forgotten. Jeanne was now singing the *Te Deum* amid all those little ones and forgotten ones, on whom were shining the glory and the joy of God.

CHAPTER 9

Perfect Joy

THE "PERFECT JOY" EPISODE in the life of Saint Francis of Assisi is well known. One winter night, the *Poverello* was returning to Assisi from Perugia. Along the way, he asked his companion: "Brother Leo, do you know what perfect joy is?"

"It is probably the joy of attaining a high degree of holiness and of being an example of it," replied Leo.

"Not at all. That is not perfect joy."

"Could it be making converts by the hundreds?"

"No," said Francis. "That is not perfect joy either."

"Is it perhaps knowing the Scriptures thoroughly, having the gift of tongues or miracles or prophecy?"

"Less still!" exclaimed Francis. "Perfect joy is not in any of these things. Should we know all science and speak all languages, and were we able to raise the dead, we would still not know perfect joy."

"Please tell me, then, what perfect joy is."

"Listen, Brother Leo. We shall soon arrive at the monastery of Saint Mary of the Angels, drenched and chilled to the bone, having eaten nothing all day. We knock at the door. The porter calls out to us from inside: 'Who are you?' We reply: 'We are two of your brothers.' He shouts louder still: 'That's not true. You are ne'er-do-wells and thieves. There's no room for you here. Go away!' And, refusing to open the door, he leaves us there in the icy rain and the night. And as we repeat our entreaties and plead with him, he comes out armed with a club, pounces on us, rolls us about in the mud and the snow, and beats us up with every knot in his stick.

"If we bear this with great patience, without being troubled or murmuring, mindful of the sufferings of the blessed Christ, there, Brother Leo, is perfect joy."

Jeanne Jugan, who was so close to Francis of Assisi in her spirit of simplicity, also knew perfect joy in her own way. Throughout her life at La Tour, she was left outside the door of the council of which she was a member, relegated to the rank of novice. She was destined to experience perfect joy even in death. The day she passed away, the first person to be informed of her demise was surely Father Le Pailleur, as superior general. The day happened to be August 28, the feast of Saint Augustine, and therefore Father Auguste Le Pailleur's own feast day. Its solemnity must not be disturbed, nor its radiance dulled. The news of Jeanne's death was therefore kept hidden until the next day, as if it were something that could wait.

Two days later, Father Le Pailleur wrote a circular letter to all the houses of the congregation. He thanked the Little

Sisters and their elderly charges for the good wishes they had sent him on the occasion of the feast of Saint Augustine. The death of Jeanne, humble foundress, was not mentioned in the letter. Forgotten in life, she was also to be forgotten in death. No one was to talk of her. No one was to remember her.

Let us wager that at dawn that day, in the grounds of La Tour, at the quiet hour of dew-fall, a teardrop formed on a small rose. No person noticed it; only the angels saw it. The small rose was weeping, but it was a tear of joy. Jeanne was in the light. The shadow of the world could no longer reach her.

Conclusion

"This strange mystery into which God has withdrawn." [1]

WHAT IS EXCEPTIONAL IN Jeanne Jugan's life is not that she was sidelined for so long, subjected to official rejection that doomed her to solitude, inactivity, and oblivion. Such situations are all too frequent, practically banal in the corridors of power and in the life of any society. Jeanne was neither the first nor the last to experience such a fate. The heavens of power cannot support two suns. Any other source of light that might threaten the brilliance of the one must be removed and hidden away. It is not only the desert that is monotheistic; power is also. Power acknowledges only one god. And, if need be, it will create a desert around itself. [2]

---

1. Blaise Pascal, letter to Charlotte de Roannez.
2. Such a way of understanding and exercising power bears no relation to the Gospel; it is diametrically opposed to the spirit of the Gospel. And it would be wrong to invoke the holiness that Jeanne Jugan derived

What is exceptional in Jeanne is above all the quality of her suffering. She suffers not from being dispossessed, rejected, forgotten, but because she can no longer approach the poor and freely express her love for them. She suffers because she can no longer pour all her energies into the project, as when she crisscrossed western France to open homes or go to the aid of those already in existence.

Jeanne's suffering cannot be understood without taking the measure of her deep and intense love for the poor, particularly for the abandoned elderly. It took the form of a burning inner urgency that consumed her. It was a divine generosity, bursting to be bestowed on the world. This was not only the love of one human being for her underprivileged neighbors. Through Jeanne was expressed the very love of God for humanity. Jeanne's suffering was that divine flame suddenly diverted from its goal, a flame a night wind persistently tried to extinguish. Here we touch upon what is truly extraordinary and unique in her experience.

The quality of her suffering is echoed by the quality of her silence. Jeanne could have shouted her suffering from the rooftops. How appropriate, how just! Her cry would have given voice to a noble and magnificent passion. Hers

---

from it in an attempt to justify or even simply excuse such practice. Thankfully, some of the Sisters' surprise and indignation at Father Le Pailleur's increasingly authoritarian behavior were finally heard in high places. It is regrettable that it should not have been heard earlier. Only several years after Jeanne's death was an apostolic inquiry set up. In 1890, Auguste Le Pailleur, aged seventy-eight, having exercised power for more than forty years, was summoned to Rome. He lived out his days in a convent. The fact that he had put his organizational skills at the service of the budding congregation cannot be forgotten, but his behavior betrays a psychological imbalance that led him to focus all the power and notoriety on himself, at the expense of truth.

would have been not the bitter cry of the offended, in revolt at being humiliated and forgotten, but the cry of a love greater than the person herself. And that cry would have been heard. The journalists who had introduced Jeanne to the public would not have failed to provide an echo for it. All it would have taken was one cry.

Instead of that, silence. Awesome and disconcerting silence. Not a word of protest, not one piece of writing, not one letter in twenty-seven years. All we have in Jeanne's hand is a single signature at the foot of an official document recording the decision by the congregation not to accept any fixed income. That is all. True enough, some of Jeanne's words have been reported to us. Apart from a few brief allusions in veiled terms, they reveal nothing of her inner tragedy.

Yet there is silence, immense and deep like the sea. In a world like ours, bombarded by the media with torrents of words, comments, accusations, and justifications of all sorts, this silence is not without surprise and challenge for us.

Jeanne confided to a young sister one day: "She who holds her tongue keeps her soul." Her silence was her soul, the flame inside her. Her silence was not a wall enclosing her within herself. On the contrary, it was a place of welcome and listening, a deeper and wider openness to all calls from God and from humanity.

It was a silence of growth. I quoted earlier the Zairian proverb: "A single tree makes much noise as it falls, but no one hears the growing of the forest." Such was the nature of Jeanne's silence. Her whole being was growing. Her silence had nothing to do with nostalgic and sterile ruminations on the past. Every day, it brought something new to the core of her being. It was the silence of the growing tree, the silence of the rose blooming freely on the grounds of La Tour. Rising sap. A creative force.

Indeed, Jeanne was not the only one who was growing. Those around her, and the universe, were growing with her. In the depths of her being, the world's chaos was turning into a dancing star and a great hymn. When, one Easter day, a group of novices burst into song after Jeanne, the very heart of the world was singing the Easter alleluia. At that moment, the Christ of our abyss became the Christ of our resurrection.

Jeanne's silent life at La Tour resembles a Japanese print. With a few delicate, precise brush strokes on a canvas appears, ethereal, in its every detail, a blossoming bough. The branch does not fill the space on the painting. It is like an island of light in the middle of an ocean. Wide expanses stretch out around it, not as a void but as an abundance of spaces: spaces for recollection, for wonder. It seems that as it flowers, the branch opens up around it expanses of ecstasy. So it is with Jeanne's life: a few words on a vast background of silence. Far from rending the silence, these words give it greater intensity by hinting at a fullness of meaning they themselves cannot express.

What is the full meaning? What is the inner song?

Through her silence, Jeanne tells us first that a person's greatness does not depend on her place in society, or on her role in it, or on social success. All those things can be taken away overnight. They can all disappear in an instant. A person's greatness resides in what is left to her precisely when everything that gave her outer brilliance has faded away. And *what* is left? Her inner resources—nothing else.

In her letters from Westerbork—the camp where Dutch Jews were detained while awaiting deportation to extermination camps—Etty Hillesum wrote:

> Among those who get washed up on this arid stretch of moor 500 meters by 600 can also be found stars of the political and cultural life of the cities. Around them, the theater sets that protected them have been swept away at a stroke by a mighty force, and here they are, still trembling and disorientated, on this stage which is bare and exposed to the winds, named Wester-bork. Torn away from their context, their silhouettes still carry the palpable aura that attaches itself to the eventful life of a society more complex than this one.
>
> They walk alongside the thin barbed wire, their vulnerable figures silhouetted, life-size, against the vast expanse of the sky. You have to have seen them walking thus....
>
> The sturdy armor forged for them by their social position, fame, and fortune has shattered around them, leaving them wearing only the thin shirt of their humanity. They find themselves in an empty space, bounded only by sky and earth, and which they will have to furnish from their own inner resources—that is all they have left.[3]

Humanity's greatness, its true wealth, does not reside in what is visible. It lies in what is carried in the heart. That is what Jeanne's silence tells us. It also tells us that a person who has been condemned to oblivion can carry the whole world in her heart: a reconciled world, already penetrated by infinite tenderness.

---

3. *Letters from Westerbork*. Originally published in the Netherlands as *Het denkende hart van de barak* (The Thinking Heart of the Barracks) by De Haan/Unieboeck b.v., Bussum, 1982.

Jeanne's silence has greater depth. Indeed, it cannot be separated from God's mystery, which she never ceased contemplating during the twenty-seven years of her confinement. We always end up resembling the object of our contemplation. Jeanne's silence reflects God's silence. It introduces us into "this strange mystery into which God has withdrawn."[4] At this point the silence takes on a prophetic dimension for our times.

Today God, the Founder of the world, also finds himself sidelined, forgotten at the door of all the councils where the business of the world is decided upon. He is not among the "great." He is relegated to the shadows as useless and nonexistent. He is gladly dispensed with. He is "dead," according to some. We are henceforth "in a reality where only men are present," as proclaimed by thinkers, proudly aware that they are introducing a new era for humanity, one in which man himself will make the world anew. Believing in God today has become a serious flaw in a person's thinking, even an obstacle to the advent of man.

God, the Forgotten, keeps silent. His silence is not a turning in on himself. The Founder of the world readily lets himself be stripped of all signs of power. There is in him no will to dominate or to possess. His silence is an expression of his truth, of his true greatness: "I know the plans I have for you ... plans for your welfare and not for harm, to give you a future with hope.... When you search for me, you will find me" (Jer 29:11, 13).

Jeanne's silence opens out into God's silence. Through it we glimpse its depth. That silence does not signify that

---

4. Blaise Pascal, letter to Charlotte de Roannez.

God has deserted us and keeps his distance from our daily life on earth. On the contrary, it signifies that he has come so close to us that we can only hear him by listening to our own hearts. We need to lend an ear to the mystery that resides in us. God's silence in us is the silence of the source.

Return to the source; God is there. He is my source, my beginning. He speaks to me in that part of me that connects with his eternal childhood. I am truly myself precisely where I am more than myself. There is in each of us, under a pile of rubble, a divine source that seeks only to gush forth and sing. Blessed is the man who, in his mature age, in spite of all life's wounds, rediscovers within himself the child's wonder-filled gaze and spontaneous trust in the goodness of being. That gaze, too soon forgotten, untainted by any will to possess and dominate, does not open on to another world; it awakens this world to profundity and perceives that it is freely given, as is the Creator's love.

"At dawn let me hear of your kindness," asks the psalmist of the Lord (Ps 143:8, *NAB*). It is always "at dawn" that one hears his love. In the beginning. At the source. At the time when no track yet runs through the dew, nothing distracts the eye, and the heart opens up like a rose in the silence of the rising dawn.

Appendix

Excerpts from the homily of Pope John Paul II during the ceremony of Beatification of Jeanne Jugan, Sunday, October 3, 1982:

I would like to meditate with you, and for you, on the actuality of the spiritual message of the newly blessed one.[1] Jeanne invites all of us, and I quote here from the Rule of the Little Sisters, *"to share in the beatitude of spiritual poverty, leading to that complete dispossession which commits a soul to God."* She invites us to this much more by her life than by those few words of hers which have been recorded and which are so marked by the seal of the Holy Spirit, such as these: *"It is so beautiful to be poor, to have nothing, to await all from God."* Joyfully aware of her poverty, she depended completely on Divine Providence, which she saw operative in her own life and in that of others. Still, this absolute confidence did not make her inactive. With the courage and faith that characterize the women of her native land,

---

1. Emphases are given as in the source document (Translator's note).

she did not hesitate to beg on behalf of the poor whom she cared for. She saw herself as their sister, their "Little Sister." She wanted to identify herself with all those elderly who were, often, more or less infirm and sometimes even abandoned. Is not this the Gospel in its pure form (cf. Mt 25:34–41)?

The soul of Jeanne was steeped in the mystery of Christ the Redeemer, especially in his passion and his cross. Her name in religion, Sister Mary of the Cross, is a real and moving symbol of this. From her native village of Petites-Croix (in English, Little Crosses ... was this a coincidence or a sign?) until her departure from this world on August 29, 1879, this foundress's life can be compared to *a long and fruitful Way of the Cross, lived with a serenity and joy conformable to the Gospel.* Must we not recall here that four years after the beginnings of the Work, Jeanne was the victim of unjustifiable interference extraneous to the group of her first companions? She allowed herself to be stripped of the office of superior, and a little later on she accepted to return to the Motherhouse for a retirement which was to last twenty-seven years, without the slightest complaint.

When summing up events such as these, the word "heroism" comes spontaneously to mind.... By the fact of so often repeating to the novices, *"Be little, stay little! Keep the spirit of humility, of littleness...."* Jeanne was really disclosing her own spiritual experience. In her long retirement at La Tour Saint-Joseph, many novices and Little Sisters came under her decisive influence and she left on her congregation the stamp of her spirit by *the quiet but eloquent radiance of her life.* In our day, *pride, the pursuit of efficacy, the temptation to use power*, all run rampant, and sometimes, unfortunately, even in the Church. They *become an obstacle to the coming of the Kingdom of God*. This is why the spirituality of Jeanne Jugan can *attract the followers of Christ and fill their hearts with simplicity and humility, with hope and evangelical joy...*

Jeanne Jugan has left us an apostolic message most relevant for our day. *You could say that she received from the Holy Spirit what may be called a prophetic intuition of the needs and deep desires of the elderly:* their desire to be respected, esteemed, and loved; their fear of loneliness and at the same time their wish for a certain independence and privacy; their longing to still feel themselves useful; and very often, a strong desire to deepen their life of faith and to live it all the more...

Though the structures of social security systems have done away with much of the misery of Jeanne Jugan's time, still her daughters come across great need among the elderly in many different countries today. And even where those structures do exist, they do not always provide the kind of home atmosphere the elderly so deeply desire and need for their physical and spiritual well-being.... From the start, the foundress did not want her congregation to limit itself to the west of France, but rather to become a real network of family homes where each person would be received, honored, and even, to the extent possible to each one, brought to a new widening of his or her existence....

May the beatification of their well-loved foundress impart to the Little Sisters of the Poor a new élan of fidelity to the spiritual and apostolic charism of their Mother! May the repercussions of this event, reaching to all the houses, have the effect of drawing more and more young girls throughout the world into the ranks of the Little Sisters!...

Finally, may this beatification be *a refreshing source of joy and of hope for all the aged of the world*, thanks to the witness, hereby solemnly acknowledged, of the woman who loved all of them so much in the name of Jesus Christ and his Church!

BOOKS & MEDIA

A mission of the Daughters of St. Paul

As apostles of Jesus Christ, evangelizing today's world:

We are CALLED to holiness
by God's living Word and Eucharist.

We COMMUNICATE the Gospel message
through our lives and through all
available forms of media.

We SERVE the Church
by responding to the hopes and needs
of all people with the Word of God,
in the spirit of St. Paul.

For more information visit our website:
www.pauline.org.

Pauline
BOOKS & MEDIA

The Daughters of St. Paul operate book and media centers at the following addresses. Visit, call or write the one nearest you today, or find us on the World Wide Web, www.pauline.org

CALIFORNIA

3908 Sepulveda Blvd, Culver City, CA 90230	310-397-8676
2460 Broadway Street, Redwood City, CA 94063	650-369-4230
5945 Balboa Avenue, San Diego, CA 92111	858-565-9181

FLORIDA

145 S.W. 107th Avenue, Miami, FL 33174	305-559-6715

HAWAII

1143 Bishop Street, Honolulu, HI 96813	808-521-2731
Neighbor Islands call:	866-521-2731

ILLINOIS

172 North Michigan Avenue, Chicago, IL 60601	312-346-4228

LOUISIANA

4403 Veterans Memorial Blvd, Metairie, LA 70006	504-887-7631

MASSACHUSETTS

885 Providence Hwy, Dedham, MA 02026	781-326-5385

MISSOURI

9804 Watson Road, St. Louis, MO 63126	314-965-3512

NEW JERSEY

561 U.S. Route 1, Wick Plaza, Edison, NJ 08817	732-572-1200

NEW YORK

64 W. 38th Street, New York, NY 10018	212-754-1110

PENNSYLVANIA

9171-A Roosevelt Blvd, Philadelphia, PA 19114	215-676-9494

SOUTH CAROLINA

243 King Street, Charleston, SC 29401	843-577-0175

VIRGINIA

1025 King Street, Alexandria, VA 22314	703-549-3806

CANADA

3022 Dufferin Street, Toronto, ON M6B 3T5	416-781-9131

¡También somos su fuente para libros,
videos y música en español!